Curious George DISCOVERS

Plants

Adaptation by Monica Perez

Based on the TV series teleplay written by Joe Fallon

Houghton Mifflin Harcourt Publishing Company

Boston   New York

Photographs on the cover and pages 3, 5, 7, 11, 21, 24 (top), 27, 30, and 32
courtesy of HMH/Carrie Garcia
Photographs on pages 9, 12, 15 (top and middle), 18, 23, and 24 (middle and bottom)
courtesy of Houghton Mifflin Harcourt
Photograph on page 15 (bottom) courtesy of HMH/Guy Jarvis
Photograph on page 16 courtesy of HMH/Megan Marascalco
Photograph on page 31 (background) courtesy of HMH/Victoria Smith

ISBN: 978-0-544-65142-5 (paper over board)

ISBN: 978-0-544-65163-0 (paperback)

Art adaptation by Rudy Obrero and Kaci Obrero

www.hmhco.com

Printed in China

SCP 10 9 8 7 6 5 4 3 2 1

4500579077

Have you ever wondered where the fruits and vegetables in your grocery store come from? Most of them are grown on farms far away and come by truck, train, boat, or plane. Are you curious about how vegetables and other plants grow? George is curious too.

George was enjoying market day. He liked the fresh vegetable section with its cucumbers, artichokes, beets, spinach, carrots, and onions — to name just a few! George wasn't sure where vegetables came from, but he sure loved to eat them. They had as many different tastes as shapes and colors.

"I was thinking about cooking vegetable soup tonight, George," said his friend the man with the yellow hat.

"But then I started to think of Chef Pisghetti's famous fresh vegetable soup and his spinach ravioli . . . maybe we should go his restaurant?" the man asked. "What do you think?"

Yum, thought George.

At Chef Pisghetti's restaurant, they sat at their favorite table and placed their order with Netti, the chef's wife.

"We'd both like fresh vegetable soup with extra carrots and spinach ravioli," the man ordered.

"Wait!" Chef Pisghetti cried as he emerged from the kitchen. "I am out of fresh veggies! We have finished the carrots and spinach."

George was worried. What would they have for dinner?

"Why don't you pick some more vegetables?" Netti asked.

"Would you like to come with me to pick the vegetables, Giorgio?" the chef asked. George nodded and followed him eagerly.

"We're going up to the roof!" the chef announced.

George was confused. Didn't the vegetables come from a market?

sunlight

carbon dioxide

oxygen

water

"Some veggies grow on farms far away, then travel to a store, where they sit around until you buy them," Chef explained. "But my veggies grow here." The chef proudly waved his arm at all the boxes filled with dirt.

"I pick them, I take them down to my kitchen, and they go into your belly all on the same day! That's Pisghetti fresh." George was still confused. Where were the fresh vegetables?

George watched in amazement as Chef Pisghetti grabbed a sprig of green and pulled a carrot out of the dirt.

Did you know . . .

that plants need sunlight, water, nutrients (food), air, and a safe place to grow? Sounds a lot like what you need to grow too!

"What's this?" Chef Pisghetti pulled another green sprig out of the dirt. "A weed! Weeds are bad. They soak up the water and nutrients from the soil that my veggies need to grow," the chef explained. "If I don't have fresh veggies to cook, I may have to close down!"

George wouldn't want that to happen.

"But I don't have time to pull the weeds out after working all day," Chef Pisghetti added.

That night George worried about Chef Pisghetti's weed problem. He lay in bed while the man read him a bedtime story, but he didn't pay much attention.

Before he knew it, George had an idea. He knew how he could help Chef Pisghetti.

The next morning George secretly took some gardening tools from the chef's roof and began to dig up the weeds.

He dug up every green thing he saw. He packed all those leafy greens into three trash bags and threw the bags away.

Did you know . . .

there are lots of different gardening tools? Here are some of the more common ones:

shovel – for moving large amounts of dirt or rocks

trowel – for digging smaller holes for seeds or bulbs

pruners – for clipping leaves or flowers

George was excited to see the chef's reaction in the garden later that day.

But the chef was not happy.

"Oh, no!" Chef Pisghetti exclaimed. "The weeds are gone, but all of my veggies are gone too! Who could have done this?" George felt bad. He realized that he didn't know how to tell the difference between a weed and a vegetable. Do you think you could?

Did you know . . .

weeds are plants that grow where they are not wanted? They usually grow quickly and take up space in a garden or on a farm. Weeds use up the nutrients and water that crops need to grow, so they should be removed. Even though weeds can harm crops, some are pretty, such as dandelions.

"I will have to plant all new vegetables," the chef
announced. He took out some seeds to show George.
"Can you believe this little seed will grow into a carrot?"
George shook his head. It was amazing!

The chef dug a small hole in the ground with his trowel, scooping the dirt out. He placed a seed into the hole and replaced the dirt.

"I'll water and fertilize the seeds regularly." The chef saw George's puzzled look. "Fertilize means to feed."

All-Purpose
LAWN FERTILIZER
All you need for a thicker, greener lawn!

"We will have new vegetables in three to four months," Chef said. "I won't have fresh veggies to use for cooking until then." George was curious. Why did it take so long? Maybe it didn't have to. Maybe a little monkey could come to the rescue!

George ran home and took all the carrots he could find from the refrigerator.

He ran back to the roof garden and began to dig a hole where the carrot seeds had been planted. George carefully placed one fully grown carrot in each hole that he dug. It took a long time, but finally George finished putting all the carrots he had brought from home in the ground. He put the tools back where he found them.

The next morning, Chef Pisghetti found a big surprise!

"My carrots grew this big overnight! It's a miracle," the chef called out.

When George arrived later in the day, Chef Pisghetti was still talking about the carrots.

"Now I won't have to close the restaurant, Giorgio, because I will have fresh veggies."

The chef scratched his head. "I wonder why the eggplants and squash didn't grow."

Oops. George had forgotten all about them.

"Tonight I will plants peas," Chef Pisghetti said. "I hope it works again!"

Explore Further

Canned or frozen or fresh? During the winter months, when fresh produce is not in season, canned or frozen vegetables can be just as healthy as fresh produce. That's because ripe vegetables are canned or frozen very soon after they are picked so they stay nutritious. If fresh vegetables have to travel a long way to the store, they may lose some of their nutrients before you eat them.

George left as soon as he could to get more vegetables from his refrigerator. He found fresh eggplants and squash, but no peas. He looked in the cupboards. There were plenty of canned peas. Can you guess what George is going to do?

The next morning the chef found fresh eggplants and squash in his garden, along with canned peas! He called to his wife, "It happened again, Netti. And the peas are in cans! It's magic! Call the TV news!"

The chef was so excited, he asked his scientist friends to come and study the special dirt in his garden.

At home, the man with the yellow hat discovered that all the vegetables in the kitchen were missing. "George," he called, "do you know what happened to all our veggies?" George nodded. He led his friend out of the house and over to Chef Pisghetti's.

When the man arrived at the rooftop garden, he finally understood what George had done.

"Well, it looks like George has been your magic gardener," the man explained. "All our vegetables have been going into your dirt."

"Ah, Netti, our garden isn't magic after all," the chef said sadly.

"But your cooking still is," Netti replied.

"Absolutely!" everyone agreed.

"That's right," said the man, "you can cook up our vegetables any day!"

Everyone helped pick the vegetables, and Chef Pisghetti invited all his friends to stay for a delicious lunch of vegetable soup. George's plan was a success after all!

Drink Up!

You already learned that a plant needs sunlight, air, water, and a good place to grow. Plants use these things to make their own food. They get most of the water they need by soaking it up from the soil through their roots and stems. Try this exciting experiment to see how plants absorb water and nutrients.

You will need . . .

- 4 glasses
- water
- red, yellow, blue, and green food coloring
- 4 Napa cabbage leaves or white flowers (such as carnations or daisies)

What to do:

1. Fill your glasses halfway up with water.
2. Pour a generous amount of a different colored food dye into each glass (make sure the water is very brightly colored!).
3. Add a single cabbage leaf or flower to each glass.
4. Let your plants sit overnight so that they have plenty of time to absorb some of the colorful water. You may want to take before and after photos. Check out the amazing results the next day! You can see how the water was absorbed by the plant by the way the food coloring has spread through it. Isn't science lovely?

Veggies All Year Round

How many different vegetables are there? Too many to list! But there are some veggies that you can easily find each season. Look at the lists below and count how many you've tried. Which are your favorites? Can you try one new vegetable every week? You can find lots of yummy recipes online.

Winter	Spring	Summer	Fall
Beets	Artichokes	Bell Peppers	Cabbage
Brussels Sprouts	Asparagus	Cucumbers	Cauliflower
Leeks	Broccoli	Eggplant	Collard Greens
Onions	Carrots	Green Beans	Ginger
Parsnips	Celery	Lima Beans	Kale
Lettuce	Garlic	Mushrooms	Peas
Mushrooms	Corn	Onions	Potatoes
Pumpkins	Rhubarb	Okra	Radishes
Rutabagas	Swiss Chard	Summer Squash & Zucchini	Spinach
Winter Squash	Turnips	Tomatoes	Sweet Potatoes and Yams

Make Your Own Vegetable Soup

Not only is vegetable soup delicious, but it's also nutritious! Ask a grownup to help you prepare this simple recipe. Feel free to try different combinations of vegetables and add your own favorites — what a great way to eat more veggies!

You will need . . .

- 2 tablespoons olive oil
- 1 medium onion, chopped
- 2 medium carrots, peeled and sliced
- 1 rib celery, sliced

- 4 cups of chicken or vegetable stock
- 1 can of diced tomatoes
- 1 cup of chopped green (or wax) beans
- 1 cup frozen peas
- 1 cup of corn kernels

What to do:

1. Cook the onion, carrot, and celery in the oil in a medium-size pot for five minutes.
2. Add broth, diced tomatoes and their juices, beans, peas, and corn. Simmer for 20–30 minutes, or until vegetables are tender. Season with salt and pepper.
3. Serve with soup crackers or some yummy bread.